better together*

* This book is best read together, grownup and kid.

 **akidsco.com**

a kids book about

TEAMS

by AJ Thomas

A Kids Co.
Editor Emma Wolf
Designer Jelani Memory
Creative Director Rick DeLucco
Studio Manager Kenya Feldes
Sales Director Melanie Wilkins
Head of Books Jennifer Goldstein
CEO and Founder Jelani Memory

DK
Delhi Technical Team Bimlesh Tiwary Pushpak Tyagi, Rakesh Kumar
Senior Production Editor Jennifer Murray
Senior Production Controller Louise Minihane
Senior Acquisitions Editor Katy Flint
Acquisitions Project Editor Sara Forster
Managing Art Editor Vicky Short
Managing Director, Licensing Mark Searle

First American edition, 2025
Published in the United States by DK Publishing, 1745 Broadway, 20th Floor,
New York, NY 10019

First published in Great Britain in 2025 by
Dorling Kindersley Limited, 20 Vauxhall Bridge Road, London SW1V 2SA
A Penguin Random House Company

The authorised representative in the EEA is
Dorling Kindersley Verlag GmbH. Arnulfstr. 124, 80636 Munich, Germany

A catalog record for this book is available from the Library of Congress.
A CIP catalogue record for this book is available from the British Library.
ISBN: 978-0-2417-4361-4

DK books are available at special discounts when purchased in bulk for sales
promotions, premiums, fund-raising, or education use. For details, contact:
DK Publishing Special Markets, 1745 Broadway, 20th Floor, New York, NY 10019
SpecialSales@dk.com

Printed and bound in China
www.dk.com
akidsco.com

This is for my team in life, who give me strength and remind me every day of the things I'm truly grateful for:

my husband, Michael, my darling daughter, Ava, and my beautiful boys, Jet and Mason—I love being on our team.

Intro for grownups

Hello, big dreamers and tiny team players! Have you ever imagined what it's like to mix and merge superpowers? Well, that's the magic of teams!

This book is my gift to you, to show that teams can be as diverse as the colors in a rainbow. They come in different shapes, sizes, numbers, and hues, each bringing its unique sparkle. I wrote this book to remind everyone that when we come together, no matter our differences, our combined superpowers make the impossible, possible.

So, grownups and kids, let's journey through these pages and celebrate the wondrous world of teams. The ones we're on, and the roles we play in them. Because when we choose to have courage, get curious, connect, and be kind, our shared superpowers light up the world!

Knock, knock...

Who's there?

Spell.

Spell, who?

OK, OK, W-H-O.

HA, HA,

HA, HA!

What did you think of my joke?

Was it funny, interesting, or did you roll your eyes?

Well, whatever you thought
of the joke, guess what?

**You just learned
something from me!**

I love jokes and making people laugh.

And I don't always
take things seriously.

But there is so much more to who I am.

I was born in Kuwait.

I was raised in
the Philippines.

I am the first in my family
to go to college in the US.

I am a first-generation immigrant.

I've been homeless and
lived in my car.

I've also worked to build some
of the best teams in the
top technology companies
around the world.

Today, I'm a wife, a mom,
a sister, and a singer.

I could keep going, but I think you get it—I've been a lot of different things throughout my life.

And I think that's what makes me a great member of a team.

Since I've done so many things, I have **a lot to offer.**

Now, you might think
you know what a team is,
but **there's so much
more to explore...**

Because, really, a team is any group of people who use curiosity, courage, connection, and kindness to solve something **together**.

That's a lot, I know, but **let me explain**.

So the first thing to know is...

TEAM EVERY

S ARE
WHERE!

Teams can be...

Friends.

Sports.

Families.

Companies.

Schools.

Governments.

Communities.

And any place where shared passions and interests exist.

Teams come in many shapes, sizes, numbers, and colors.

ISN'T THAT AMAZING!?

You might not realize this, but you're already a part of so **many teams**.

Don't believe me? Well...

Do you love recess?

Do you hang out with your family?

Do you play in the chess club?

Do you think about your goals?

Do you share things you've learned?

Do you ask big questions
about the universe?

Do you feel a part of something
that's bigger than you?

All of these are ways
of being on a team.

You see, I've been a part of multiple teams and **didn't even realize it**.

Whether I was a cheerleader, part of the marching band, a member of a local sports team, a singer in a band, or an older sister to my siblings, I was on a team.

Each team looked different and so did my roles within them.

Sometimes, I led the team and it was my job to make things happen.

Other times, I supported someone else's needs.

Most of the time, I used my abilities to help our team achieve our goals.

Can you think of teams **you're on**?

WHAT DO YOU

ROLES PLAY?

What are some goals you want to achieve on these teams?

It might seem silly to call all these things teams—but that's really **what they are!**

Because no one ever truly does anything alone.

And teams are capable of **incredible things** when they use their superpowers together.

Every **great team** has the same 4 ingredients.

Are you ready to hear them?

First is...

CURIOSITY.

Exploring things about your teammates and your shared goals is very important.

Curiosity can look like giving a shout-out to someone on your team who is stellar at what they do.

It can also look like asking a teammate what success looks like for them.

And it definitely looks like being available to answer questions when they are unsure.

Second is...
COURAGE.

Being able to speak up and offer your skill sets when you are a part of a team is essential.

Courage can look like telling the team about something new you learned.

It can also look like offering help if you see someone struggling.

And it definitely looks like calling out achievements, or when something feels broken or confusing.

Third is... CONNECTION.

Once you get to know your teammates and each person's talents, it's crucial to connect that knowledge to your shared goals.

Connection can look like creating chore lists with your family.

It can look like clarifying the goal of your assignments at school.

And it definitely looks like being able to work together, as a team, wherever you're going next.

Fourth is...

KINDNESS.

Being kind is another important ingredient of great teams—because not everyone does everything perfect all the time.

Kindness can look like not being too hard on yourself if you make a mistake.

It can also look like having patience or encouraging someone when they don't get something right on the first try.

And it definitely looks like being there for each other when times are good and when times get tough.

They are capable of so much when everyone comes together for a **shared purpose**.

You'll be a part of so many teams throughout your life.

And **you won't be** on every team forever.

Because maybe some new team **needs you** even more!

So, what **teams** are you on?

What **roles** do you play in them?

And what **goals** are you trying to achieve?

YOUR

Draw these circles on a piece

TEAM B

What are your goals?
What are your roles?

TEAM A

What are your goals?
What are your roles?

TEAMS!

of paper and use the questions within to brainstorm.

TEAM D

What are your goals?
What are your roles?

TEAM C

What are your goals?
What are your roles?

Go, teams!

Outro for grownups

Teams are everywhere! I hope you found this book helpful and inspiring, and that you're able to encourage others to think about what teams they might be on. Great things are rarely accomplished by 1 person, all on their own. Great things always happen when there are teams involved.

Remember, every great team has the same 4 ingredients: curiosity, courage, connection, and kindness. Use these ingredients to build strong teams and achieve great things!

About The Author

AJ Thomas (she/her) belongs to many teams. She's a wife, daughter, mom, sister, and a singer in a band. She currently serves as an advisor to early stage startups, CEOs, and founders on how to build world-class teams.

AJ wrote this book to remind us that teams are everywhere! Growing up, AJ moved from country to country, adapting quickly to changing circumstances. Over the years, she realized the best work happens in teams—not individually. Whether as a family member, within a group of good friends, on a sports team, or a part of a mission-focused group of people, each team shares 4 superpowers that when combined, create something powerful!

This book is meant to serve as a reminder that curiosity, courage, connection, and kindness can go a long way in accomplishing something great.

 @helloajthomas   @itsajthomas   helloajthomas.com

Made to empower.

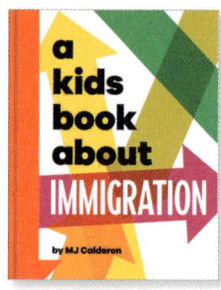
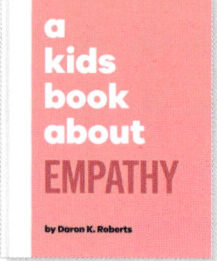

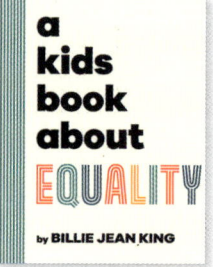

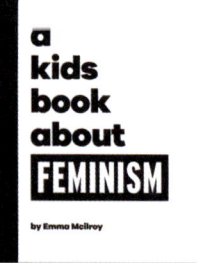
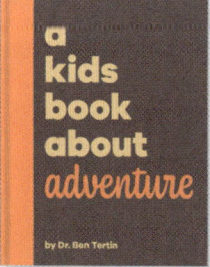

Discover more at akidsco.com